by Amy Jordan Smith

Life Is Short. Eat Biscuits!

Published by:

Santa Monica Press LLC
P.O. Box 1076
Santa Monica, CA 90406-1076
1-800-784-9553
www.santamonicapress.com
books@santamonicapress.com

Printed in China

Library of Congress Cataloging-in-Publication Data

Smith, Amy Jordan, 1958-
Life is short, eat biscuits! / by Amy Jordan Smith ; illustrated by Ted Meyer.
p. cm.
ISBN 1-891661-41-8
1. Dogs--Humor. I. Title.

PN6231.D68S65 2004
818'.602--dc22

2003028000

Introduction

Calvin "Boo Boo" Smith came into my life one day when a friend of mine said, "I found a stray dog around the house, but Mary says no more animals. Keep him until I find his owner."

"Sure, Bern," I replied.

So I took home a ragged runt of a buff-colored cocker spaniel who, it turned out, had heartworms, a double dose of ear infections, an indomitable will to live and the cutest, goofiest grin I ever saw on a dog.

It was late that first night I brought him home. Showing him the layout of my second floor apartment and his new foster home, I opened the sliding glass door and took him out on the balcony. Without a tentative step he walked right through the railing to wander around on the screen roof of the unit below me

"Here doggie, doggie," I begged on my hands and knees. He was just out of reach and all I could think of was calling Bern: *You know that dog you gave me....*

Finally, he came within reach and I grabbed him. "Bad dog," I said.

He licked my face and owned me immediately.

That was the last time Calvin was allowed on the balcony without my complete attention and a leash, except for the evening he slipped out behind me as I closed the door. It was raining like, well, cats and dogs, and he managed to walk over the screen roof and onto to the balcony next door. A few minutes later I was going crazy because I couldn't find the dog. He was just here. *How can you lose a dog in an apartment that's only 1,000 square feet!*

Right about the time I thought I had flat gone mad, my neighbor, Mr. Donaldson, knocked on the door and asked if I were looking for Calvin. It seems the Donaldsons were having cocktails when Mrs. Donaldson looked out through her sliding glass door and screamed. Calvin had walked across the roof screen and onto their balcony to get out of the rain.

"Yes, that's my wet dog."

We had a good laugh, and I suppose Mrs. Donaldson had another cocktail.

Typical Calvin. Some might have called him dim, but what he lacked in smarts he made up for in kind and gentle character. He was no doubt the happiest dog I've ever known. His tail always wagged, though perhaps a little faster when you called his name for a walk or if a biscuit were in sight.

Through the years we looked after one another. As his health began to fail, I wrote down everything he taught me about loving and living, his legacy of sorts. I didn't actually write it for him, though, because Calvin was a natural and he had long since solved the fundamental mysteries of life and was content to rest on a cool tile floor until the next belly rub. No, this book was written for me and others like me who know the unconditional love of a good dog never wavers—it is faithful and warm and true.

You could say these pages contain everything my dog taught me about being happy, and I didn't even have to ask for the lessons.

It's a dog's life. We should all live the better for it.

Calvin is now in Pet Heaven, and I still miss him. He's buried with his favorite toys and a couple of biscuits, under a palm tree and next to a dog named Happy. His stone reads "Life Is Short. Eat Biscuits!"

Sometimes, in a particular moment, I feel his Zen and imagine his wet nose next to mine, a paw brushing against my hand, nudging me along to reach for a biscuit.

Amy J. Smith

www.eatbiscuits.com

Be the biscuit.

Learn a firm paw shake.

Dogs have a long memory
for good things
and a short memory
for bad things.

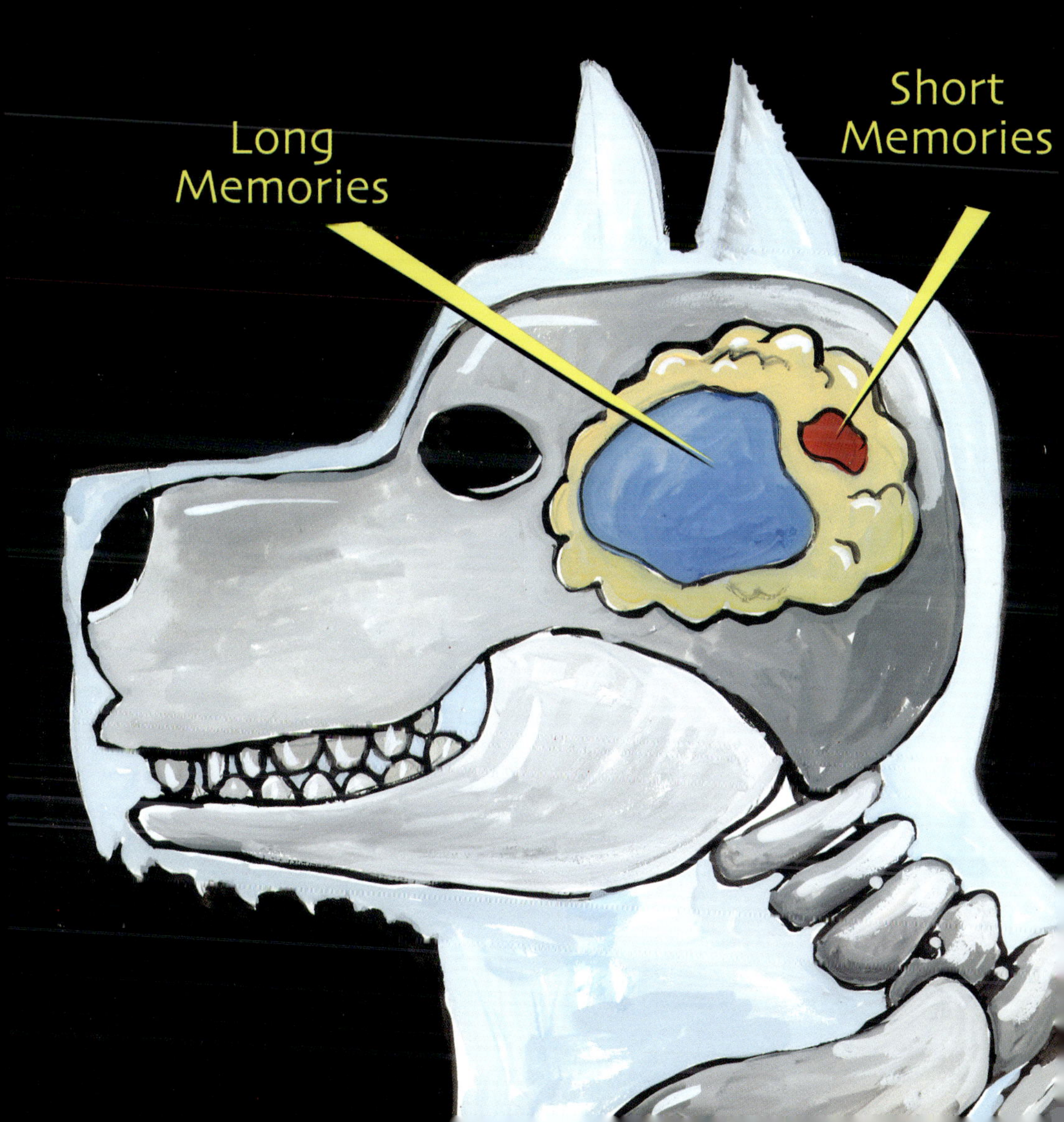
Long
Memories
Short
Memories

It's a real talent
to be able to hear
a refrigerator door open
in the middle of the night
while sound asleep.
You must first learn
to listen with your eyes closed.

Ever notice
a three-legged dog
acts as if he still
has four legs?

For a dog
there is only do
or not do.

If you really believe
you'll get a biscuit,
you will.

Every dog has his day.

Indeed.

Play nice with other dogs.

Walk with your head up
and your tail wagging.

Don't count your biscuits
before they are in your paw,
but once you have them,
savor every bite.

BISCUITS

No matter where you go,
remember the way home.

If you are in the dog house...

...redecorate.

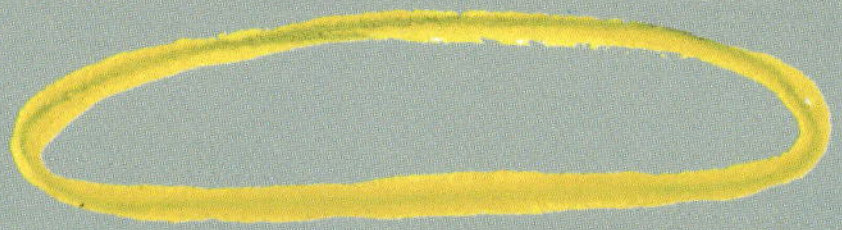

Good dogs
get more biscuits
and belly rubs
than bad dogs.

For a dog,
every moment,
this moment,
is the moment.

Sing from your heart.

When a dog
wants something,
he asks for it.

If it looks like a cat
and walks like a cat
and talks like a cat,
it's a cat.

Woof
Woof
Woof
Woof
Woof
Woof

Bark loudly
if you sense danger.

Growl if danger
comes too close.

GRRRR
GRRRR
GRRRR

If you absolutely
have to fight,
bite to win.

Life is short.
Eat biscuits!

If it makes
your tail wag,
it's good.

If it makes
you throw up,
it's bad.

Take your medicine
with a biscuit.
It will be easier
to swallow.

Believe it or not,

you will feel better

after a bath.

If you bury a bone,
remember where
you put it.

Learn to sit, stay,

heel, and fetch.

HOW TO
Sit,
Stay
Heel &
Fetch

Always save a biscuit
for a rainy day.

Play is good.

Sometimes all you need
is a rub on the belly . . .
or a pat on the head.

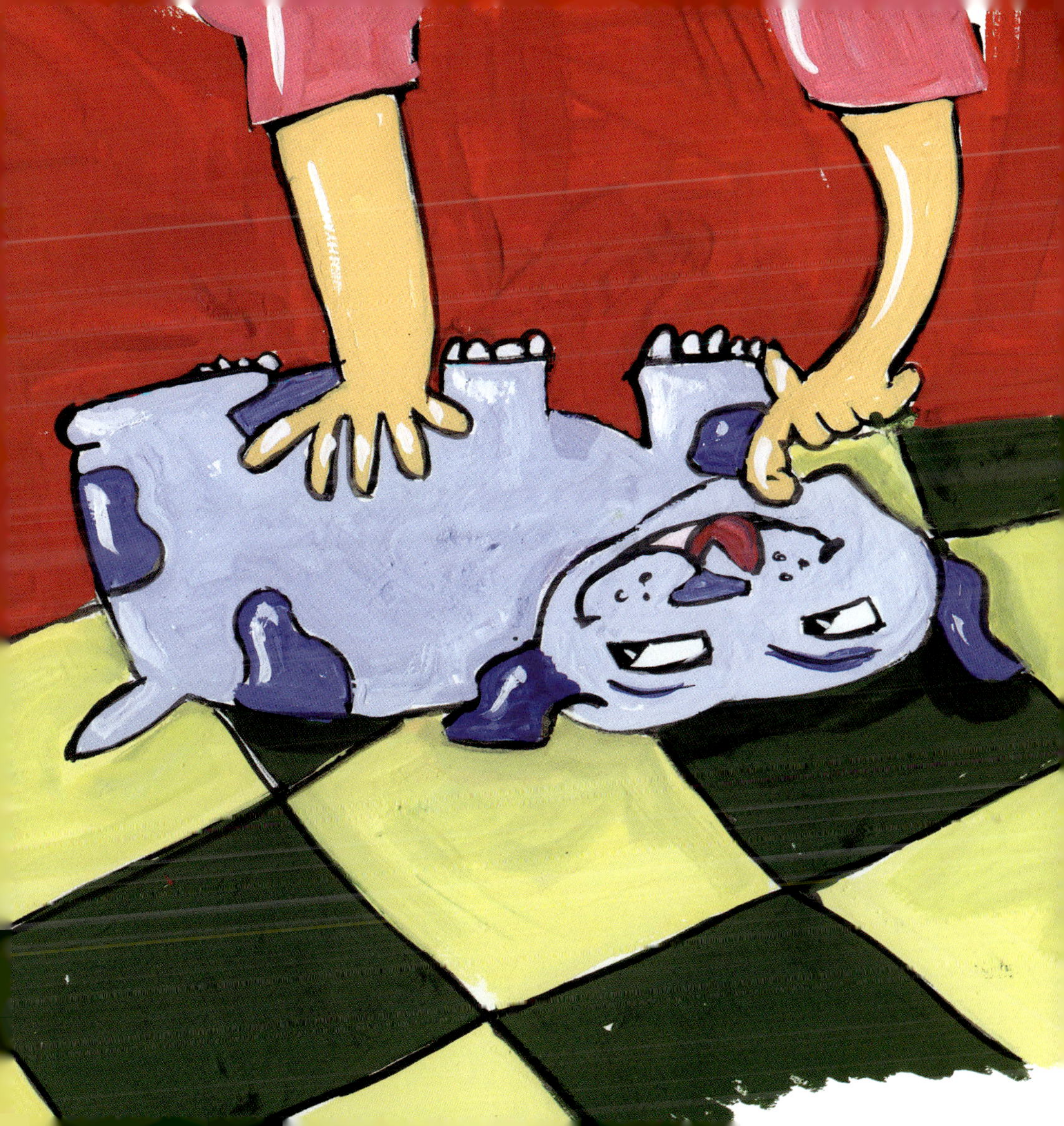

Bark at yourself
every once in awhile.

A dog lives her life
in the present tense.
This is a good thing.

Behind every cloud
is the sun
and a biscuit.

Sometimes all it takes
to make someone happy
is a cold nose
and a wet lick on the cheek.

Make friends
with the pack.

It doesn't matter
if you're born
a mutt or a pedigree,
a good dog is a good dog.

Learn to wait patiently.

but let them know you are waiting.

Biscuits

come in all shapes

and sizes.

You can say a lot
without talking.
Ask a dog.

Go home when you're called.

Ask yourself,
"What would Lassie do?"

Be gentle with puppies—

you were one once.

Be kind to old dogs—
you will be one someday.

Good dogs,
like good memories,
live in your heart forever.

The End.